Presented to Freddie ~~Gardner~~

on the occasion of his Confirmation

With the prayers and best wishes
of all those at
Holy Trinity, Minchinhampton
and
St. Barnabas, Box

Michael Irving

Rector

Malvern College Chapel
Sunday, 7th May 2006

Prayers of Our Faith

Classic Christian Prayers

Douglas Dales

CANTERBURY
PRESS
Norwich

© Douglas Dales 2003

First published in 2003 by the Canterbury Press Norwich
(a publishing imprint of Hymns Ancient & Modern Limited,
a registered charity)
St Mary's Works, St Mary's Plain,
Norwich, Norfolk, NR3 3BH

www.scm-canterburypress.co.uk

British Library Cataloguing in Publication data

A catalogue record for this book is available
from the British Library

Bible references are adapted from
The Revised English Bible
© 1989 Oxford and Cambridge University Presses

ISBN 1-85311-529-0

Typeset by Regent Typesetting, London
Printed and bound by
Creative Print and Design, Wales

Contents

Teach Us To Pray

A child once said, 'Heaven is a very big place
because it is where God is.
But the way there is very small because
it is in our hearts.'

This book of prayers has been designed to encourage
people to pray. It can also be used as a companion to
This is My Faith, which is a book to help prepare
people for Confirmation, and to support them in
their Christian life thereafter. The first part of *Prayers
of Our Faith* follows the themes of that book quite
closely. This prayer book can be used, therefore, as a
regular part of preparation for Confirmation, either
privately or in a group. It can of course be used by
anyone of any age, and of any church. There is an
index of themes at the back of the book as an aid to
personal prayer in different situations.

How do we develop and deepen our prayer as life moves on? Just as circumstances change around us, so we also change; so too does the way we pray. These prayers and the writings that follow them reveal to us a glimpse of the depth of prayer, and the demands that God's love can make upon our lives. Something of the spirit of prayer, of holiness itself, can kindle in our hearts as we read carefully what others have written from their own experience of communion with God. For the love of God is natural to any human being who sincerely seeks Him.

It is most important to make time each day to pray on a regular basis: quality not quantity of time is what matters. A framework of prayers will support the prayers of our own hearts; the words of others will complement our own words and thoughts. Upon this framework the life of prayer and the love of God can grow. It is also important to receive Holy Communion regularly, at least twice a month; for we cannot grow in prayer on our own. Talking to other Christians, family and friends about our spiritual life can also be of real help and support.

The Bible exists to bring our hearts and minds into contact with God Himself, as we see Him in Jesus. Reading the Bible regularly and prayerfully opens a dialogue with God, and daily contact with the gospels in particular deepens our sense of who Jesus is. When we read the Bible in the light of Christ, the Holy Spirit in the depths of our heart can guide our thinking into a deeper grasp of God's truth.

It is also wise to keep some spiritual writing by a saint or some other person at hand, and at the end of this book some titles are recommended. This often helps us to make the link between the words of the Bible and our own life. It is also a real encouragement to know that others have moved along the path of prayer, and like guides and friends, their teaching and example brings to us some sense of the reality of the Holy Spirit.

Prayer is an art, learnt over a lifetime: at times it is very challenging and difficult. Sometimes we may feel that we are wandering through an arid desert, or lost in some inner darkness of soul. Do not lose heart! In the darkness shines the light of Christ: and sometimes his light can only be seen clearly in the darkness. The prayers and example of his saints and their teaching may mean most to us in such times, for they have been through these moments too, and now they rejoice in the light and love of God.

In all their diversity of history and language, these prayers and teachings about prayer are the common inheritance of the whole Church. They are also the gift of the Holy Spirit to all who seek God in Jesus Christ, with all their heart and mind, and soul and strength.

PART ONE

Prayers of Our Faith

Introduction

Prayer in response to the Bible is at the very heart of the Christian life, so in each section of Part One there is a keynote text from the Bible for thought and reflection, and then a prayer, which relates to the aspect of being a Christian that is being considered. It may be a good idea to look up the surrounding passage in the Bible from which the keynote text is taken. It may also help to have a brief time of silence and reflection between reading the Bible text and saying the prayer, privately or together. These prayers are drawn from right across the history and different traditions of the Church, including prayers by some of the saints: there is a timeline of when they lived at the back of the book.

Prayers of Our Faith

The Lord's Prayer

Our Father, who art in heaven,
Hallowed be thy Name.
Thy Kingdom come,
Thy Will be done
On earth as it is in heaven.
Give us this day our daily bread,
And forgive us our sins
As we forgive those who have sinned against us.
Lead us not into temptation,
But deliver us from evil.
For thine is the Kingdom, the Power and the Glory,
For ever and ever. Amen.

A Relationship with God

When you pray, go into a room by yourself, shut the door, and pray to your Father in secret; and your Father who sees what is done in secret will reward you.

(St Matthew 6:6)

O God, you have prepared for those who love you
Such good things as pass our understanding;
Pour into our hearts such love towards you,
That loving you in all things and above all things,
We may obtain your promises, which exceed all
    that we can desire.
We ask this through Jesus Christ our Lord. Amen.

The Call of Christ

Jesus said, 'Anyone who wants to be a follower of mine must renounce self; he must take up his cross and follow me.'

(St Mark 8:34)

Open our hearts, O Lord, to your presence within
   us,
Our ears to hear your loving call,
And our minds to discern your will.
Open our hands to receive you and to share you
   with others:
Make us true disciples and friends of your Son,
   Jesus Christ our Lord. Amen.

A Christ-like Life

God is love; those who dwell in love dwell in God, and God in them.

(1 John 4:16)

Christ, the Wisdom of God, lead us to a world of
  freedom,
To your uncreated Light,
To love, peace and freedom from anxiety.
Holy God, holy and mighty, holy and immortal,
Have mercy upon us, for we take refuge in you.
May your Holy Spirit breathe into us love and
Freedom from all fear of friend or foe,
Of the known and the unknown,
By day and night, wherever we go.
For you have commanded that our hearts should
  not be troubled;
You have given us your peace through your Holy
  Spirit,
To guide us into all truth under the protection of
  your saints. Amen.

The Way, the Truth and the Life

Jesus said, 'I am the way, the truth and the life; no one comes to the Father except by me.'

(St John 14:6)

Lord Jesus Christ, alive and at large in the world,
Help me to follow and find you there today,
In the places where I work, meet people, spend
    money and make plans.
Take me as a disciple of your kingdom,
To see others through your eyes,
And to listen to the questions you are asking
    through them;
To welcome all men and women with your trust
    and truth,
And to change the things that contradict God's
    love,
By the power of the Cross, and in the freedom of
    your Spirit. Amen.

The Challenge of Temptation

Jesus has been tempted in every way as we are, only without sinning.

(Hebrews 4:15)

O God, we are set in the midst of such dangers and
    temptations,
That because of the weakness of our human nature
We can hardly remain steady in our life and
    vocation.
Give us health of body and mind, and a true sense
    of values,
That whatever we have to endure because of our
    sins and failures,
We may overcome with your love and help.
We ask this through Jesus Christ our Lord. Amen.

The Meaning of Baptism

You are a chosen race, a royal priesthood, a dedicated
nation, a people claimed by God for His own, to
proclaim the glorious deeds of Him who has called
you out of darkness into His own marvellous light.

(1 Peter 2:9)

Lord, in your mercy save us, forgive us our mistakes,
Cleanse our sins and remedy our weaknesses.
Pour upon us the grace of Baptism, and accept our
    repentance.
Heal the sick in body, mind or spirit;
Remember our fathers and mothers, our brothers
    and sisters in Christ
And all who have died.
Pour your Holy Spirit of love and peace upon your
    world.
May we sense the prayers of your holy Mother, and
    of all your saints.
To our Lord Jesus Christ belong glory, honour and
    worship for ever. Amen.

Freedom and Light

For with you is the well of life, and in your light shall
we see light.

(Psalm 36:9)

Grant us your light, O Lord,
That the darkness in our hearts being wholly passed
    away,
We may come at last to the light that is Christ.
For Christ is the morning star,
Who when the night of this world is past,
Brings to his saints the promised light of life,
And opens to them eternal day. Amen.

(Bede)

Life in the Spirit

Jesus said, 'If anyone is thirsty, let him come to me and drink. Whoever believes in me, as scripture says, "Streams of living water shall flow from within him."'

(St John 7:37–8)

O heavenly King, O Comforter, the Spirit of truth.
You are everywhere and fill all things,
The treasure of blessing, and giver of life:
Come and abide in us, and cleanse us from all
    impurity;
And in your love and goodness save us. Amen.

The Fruit of the Spirit

The fruit of the Spirit is love, joy, peace, patience, kindness, goodness, faithfulness, gentleness, and self-control: against such there is no law.

(Galatians 5:22–3)

Lord, make us to walk in your way;
Where there is love and wisdom, there is neither
    fear nor ignorance;
Where there is patience and humility, there is
    neither anger nor annoyance;
Where there is poverty and joy, there is neither
    greed nor ambition;
Where there is peace and true prayer, there is
    neither care nor restlessness;
Where there is the fear of God to guard the heart,
    there no enemy can enter;
Where there is mercy and prudence, there is neither
    excess nor harshness;

This we know through the example of him who laid
down his life for us,
Your Son, Jesus Christ our Lord. Amen.

(St Francis)

Adoration and Worship

I saw the Lord, high and exalted, and the skirt of his robe filled the temple. Seraphim were in attendance on Him, and they were calling to one another, 'Holy, holy, holy is the Lord God of hosts; the whole earth is full of His glory.'

(Isaiah 6:1-3)

O God, the maker and re-maker of human nature,
    the Creator uncreated:
You spread the heavens and founded the earth;
You planted Paradise and formed humanity from
    the dust.
You recalled your children from error to the way of
    Life,
Giving them your Law and speaking from the midst
    of fire.
You blessed the patriarchs, and called the prophets,
For you are loving, truthful, and without deceit.

You are one and all-powerful, the fountain of
   eternal life;
You live forever with your Son, our Lord Jesus
   Christ,
And with the Holy Spirit, unto the ages of ages.
   Amen.

Repentance and Confession

The tax collector in the temple kept his distance and would not even lift up his eyes to heaven, saying, 'God, have mercy on me, sinner that I am.'

(St Luke 18:13)

We ask you, O Lord, to listen to our prayers,
And to forgive the sins of all who confess to you:
That we who stand accused by our conscience
May be absolved by your pardon, love and mercy.
We ask this through Jesus Christ our Lord. Amen.

Thanksgiving

Blessed be the God and Father of our Lord Jesus Christ, who has conferred on us in Christ every spiritual blessing in the heavenly realms.

(Ephesians 1:3)

We bless you, we praise you, we give you thanks,
We worship you in every place of your Kingdom;
For you are God, indescribable, beyond thought,
    invisible, eternal:
You and your only Son and your Holy Spirit.
You brought us out of nothing into being,
And when we fell away from you,
You raised us up again
Through the life and death and resurrection of your
    Son, Jesus Christ.
By your Holy Spirit you leave nothing undone
To bring us to heaven to share in your Kingdom of
    love.

Prayers of Our Faith

For all this we give thanks to you,
And to your only Son and to your Holy Spirit,
For all the blessings that we receive from you,
   hidden and revealed,
Now and for ever. Amen.

(Liturgy of St John Chrysostom)

Supplication and Intercession

We often do not even know how we ought to pray, but through our inarticulate yearning the Spirit himself is pleading for us; and God who searches our inmost being knows what the Spirit means, for he pleads for God's people as God Himself wills.

(Romans 8:26–7)

Almighty and everlasting God,
The comfort of the sad and the strength of those
   who suffer;
Hear the prayers of your children who cry out of
   any trouble;
And to every distressed person grant mercy, relief
   and refreshment;
Through your Son, Jesus Christ our Lord. Amen.

The Love of God

God so loved the world that he gave His only Son,
that everyone who has faith in him may not perish
but have eternal life.

(St John 3:16)

In the face of Jesus
We behold the glory of Love's power
In meekness perfected;
Love's faithful witness to the end
To bring love in where love is not,
Manifesting Love's compassion,
Love's eternal activity towards humanity;
That through his offering of the perfect life,
All those who come to him
May burn upon the altar of his love,
And one with him may dwell within the sanctuary
   of his love.

(Gilbert Shaw)

Praying with the Bible

Your word is a lamp unto my feet, and a light upon my path.

(Psalm 119:105)

Eternal Light, shine into our hearts,
Eternal Goodness, deliver us from evil,
Eternal Power, be our support,
Eternal Wisdom, scatter the darkness of our
    ignorance,
Eternal Pity, have mercy upon us:
That with all our heart and mind and soul and
    strength
We may seek your face,
And so be brought by your infinite mercy into your
    holy presence.
We ask this through Jesus Christ our Lord. Amen.

(Alcuin)

Compassion and Justice

If someone who possesses the good things of this world sees someone in need and withholds compassion from him, how can it be said that the love of God dwells in him?

(1 John 3:17)

God of love, you see all the suffering, injustice and
    misery in this world;
Have pity, we pray, on what you have created;
In your mercy look upon the poor, the oppressed
    and the destitute;
Fill our hearts with deep compassion for those who
    suffer,
And hasten the coming of your Kingdom of justice
    and truth;
For the sake of your Son, our Lord Jesus Christ.
    Amen.

Possessions and Generosity

Jesus said, 'No person can serve two masters; for either he will hate the first and love the second, or he will be devoted to the first and despise the second. You cannot serve God and Money.'

(St Matthew 6:24)

Lord Jesus Christ, Son of the living God,
Who at the last judgement will acknowledge all
    deeds of mercy as done to you: Grant that, in this
    world of sin and pain and want,
We may never pass by the poor and the helpless,
    whose cry is your own;
For the sake of your great love we ask this. Amen.

Respect and Human Rights

If you believe in our Lord Jesus Christ who reigns in glory you must always be impartial. . . . Has not God often chosen those who are poor in the eyes of the world to be rich in faith?

(James 2:1 and 5)

Lord, you have taught us that this world is yours
    and all those who dwell in it.
Hear us as we pray for the life and well-being of our
    world,
That every nation may seek the way that leads to
    peace;
That human rights and freedom may everywhere be
    respected;
That the earth's resources may be fairly and
    generously shared among all.
We ask this through your Son, Jesus Christ our
    Lord. Amen.

Sexuality and Marriage

Do you not know that your body is the temple of the indwelling Holy Spirit, and the Spirit is God's gift to you? You do not belong to yourselves; you were bought at a price. Then honour God in your body.

(1 Corinthians 6:19–20)

Almighty God, our heavenly Father,
You gave marriage to be a source of blessing to
   human beings.
We thank you for the joys of family life.
May we know your presence and peace in our
   homes.
Fill them with your love, and use them for your
   glory.
We ask this through your Son, Jesus Christ our
   Lord. Amen.

Care for Children

Jesus said, 'Whoever humbles himself and becomes like this child will be greatest in the kingdom of heaven, and whoever receives one such child in my name receives me.'

(St Matthew 18:4–5)

Heavenly Father, Maker of all things,
You enable us to share in your work of creation.
Bless us in the gift and care of children,
That our homes and schools may be places of love,
    security and truth,
And our children grow up to know and love you
In your Son, Jesus Christ our Lord. Amen.

Praying with the Saints

Worthy is the Lamb who was slain, to receive power and wealth, wisdom and might, honour and glory and praise! Praise and honour, glory and might, to Him who sits on the throne and to the Lamb for ever!

(Revelation 5:12)

Almighty and eternal God,
You kindle in the hearts of your saints the fire of
    your love.
Grant to us the same virtue of faith, love, and
    prayer.
That as we rejoice in their triumphs,
So we may be perfected after their example,
In the following of your Son, our Lord Jesus Christ.
    Amen.

Seeking God's Will

Put all your trust in the Lord, and do not rely on your own understanding. At every step you take keep Him in mind, and He will direct your path.

(Proverbs 3:5–6)

Grant me, O Lord, true and surpassing love;
Firmness of faith in my heart;
The helmet of salvation on my head;
The sign of Christ on my forehead;
The word of salvation in my mouth;
A good will in my mind;
The girdle of chastity around my instincts;
Honesty in all I do;
Responsibility in my way of life;
Humility in prosperity;
Patience in affliction;
Hope in my Creator and heavenly Father,
Love of eternal life;
Perseverance until the end.
I ask this through Jesus Christ,
My Friend and Lord and Saviour. Amen.

The Body of Christ

Christ is like a single body with its many limbs and organs, which many as they are together make up one body. For in the one Spirit we were all brought into the one body by Baptism, whether Jews or Greeks, slaves or free.

(1 Corinthians 12:12–13)

O Lord Jesus Christ, you said to your disciples,
'Peace I leave with you; my own peace I give unto
    you.'
Regard not our sins, but the faith of your Church:
And grant us that peace and unity which is agreeable
    to your will.
For you live and reign with the Father and the Holy
    Spirit,
One God for ever. Amen.

Abiding in Christ

Jesus said, 'I am the true vine: dwell in me, as I in you. No branch can bear fruit by itself, but only if it remains united with the vine; no more can you bear fruit, unless you remain united with me.'

(St John 15:1–4)

O God, by whose Spirit the whole body of the
    Church is guided and sanctified;
Preserve in us the grace of holiness
For the new life which you have given to your
    family;
That renewed in mind and body,
And maintaining unity in the faith,
We may abide in you, and worthily serve you.
We ask this through Jesus Christ our Lord. Amen.

The Good Shepherd

Jesus said, 'I have come that people may have life,
and may have it in all its fullness. I am the good shepherd; the good shepherd lays down his life for the
sheep.'

(St John 10:10–11)

Almighty God, our Lord Jesus Christ,
You stretched out your pure and loving hands on
    the Cross for us,
And redeemed us with your holy and precious
    blood:
Enable me so to feel and understand this mystery
That I may attain true repentance,
And unfailing perseverance all the days of my life.
    Amen.

Time in God's Presence

O God, you are my God; I seek you eagerly with a heart that thirsts for you, for your unfailing love is better than life itself.

(Psalm 63:1–3)

Gracious and Holy Father,
Give us wisdom to perceive you,
Diligence to seek you,
Patience to wait for you,
Eyes to behold you,
A heart to meditate on you,
And a life to proclaim you;
Through the power of the Spirit
Of your Son, Jesus Christ our Lord. Amen.

(St Benedict)

Sensing God's Reality

When the Lord saw that Moses had turned aside to look at the burning bush, He called to him out of the bush; and Moses hid his face, for he was afraid to look at God.

(Exodus 3:4–6)

Most high and glorious God,
Come and enlighten the darkness of our hearts.
Give us true faith, a certain hope, and a perfect
    love.
Give us a sense of your divine presence
And true knowledge of yourself,
So that we may do everything in fulfilment of your
    holy will;
We ask this through your Son, Jesus Christ our
    Lord. Amen.

(St Francis)

The Mind in the Heart

Lord, my heart is neither proud nor conceited; but I am calm and quiet like a child clinging to its mother.

(Psalm 131:1–2)

Lord Jesus Christ, our Judge and Saviour,
Set before us the vision of your purity,
And let us see our sins in the light of your holiness.
Pierce our self-contentment with your burning love,
And let that love consume all that hinders us from
  the perfect service of you;
For as your holiness is our judgement,
So your wounds are our salvation. Amen.

(William Temple)

Evil and the Challenge of Good

What can separate us from the love of Christ? Can affliction or hardship, persecution, hunger, naked-ness, danger, or the sword? I am convinced that nothing in all creation can separate us from the love of God in Jesus Christ our Lord.

(Romans 8:35–9)

Christ the true Light, who enlightens the whole
   creation,
Fill us with the joy of your light and love.
O radiance of the Father, pure and holy one,
   dwelling in light,
Drive from us all evil passions and ill feelings;
Protect us from all harm and spiritual attack.
Grant us to live according to your commandments
   in purity of heart;
Grant us your mercy and hope on the day of
   resurrection. Amen.

One Humanity in Christ

There is no such thing as Jew and Greek, slave and freeman, male and female: for you are all one in Christ Jesus.

(Galatians 3:28)

God our Father, you have made all men and women
   in your likeness,
And you love everyone whom you have made;
Suffer not our human family to separate itself from
   you,
By building barriers of race, religion and colour.
As your Son our Saviour was born of a Jewish
   mother,
Rejoiced in the faith of a Syrian woman and of a
   Roman soldier,
Welcomed the Greeks who sought him,
And permitted a person from Africa to carry his
   Cross,

So teach and enable us to regard the members of all
   races
As fellow-heirs of your love and of your kingdom.
We ask this for the sake of your Son, Jesus Christ
   our Lord. Amen.

The Cost of Discipleship

Let us run with resolution the race which lies ahead
of us, our eyes fixed on Jesus, the pioneer and
perfecter of our faith. For the sake of the joy that lay
ahead of him, he endured the Cross, ignoring its
disgrace, and has taken his seat at the right hand of
the throne of God.

(Hebrews 12:1–2)

Give us, Lord, the determination, which no
    unworthy affection can sap;
Give us the strength, which no affliction can
    undermine;
Give us the integrity, which nothing unworthy of
    you can destroy.
Pour upon us your Holy Spirit so that we may receive
Understanding to know you,
Persistence to seek you,
Wisdom to find you,
Faithfulness in the end to embrace you;
Through your Son, Jesus Christ our Lord. Amen.

(St Thomas Aquinas)

Goodness and Human Dignity

Jesus said, 'I give you a new commandment: love one another; as I have loved you, so you are to love one another.'

(St John 13:34)

Heavenly Father, your love embraces all the nations upon earth;
Free us from racial prejudice, and the denial of human goodness and dignity.
Draw us by the death of your Son upon the Cross
Into one true fellowship of men and women of all races and languages;
That justice, mercy and peace may be established everywhere.
We ask this through Jesus Christ our Lord. Amen.

Other Faiths

The king will answer the righteous: 'Truly I tell you: anything you did for one of my brothers or sisters here, however insignificant, you did for me.'

(St Matthew 25:40)

God and Father of all human beings,
In your love you have made all the nations of the
    world to be one family.
Help those of different races and religions to love
    and understand one another better.
Take away hatred, jealousy and prejudice,
So that loving you more deeply
We may work together for the coming of your
    kingdom of righteousness and peace.
We ask this through your Son, Jesus Christ our
    Lord. Amen.

(Evelyn Underhill)

The Eucharist

Every time you eat this bread and drink this cup, you proclaim the death of the Lord until he comes.

(1 Corinthians 11:26)

Lord Jesus Christ, the way, the truth and the life:
We seek eternal life that you may make us your
  friends.
You came from heaven to pour life into the world;
We know you to be the bread of life, the loving
  bond of human hearts.
One who comes to you will never suffer hunger.
One who believes in you will never thirst.
By the mystery of this Eucharist you redeem us from
  death,
So that we may live in you more securely and wisely.
You, Christ, are our teacher to whom we draw near
  in love:
May your love become the foundation of our hearts
  and minds,

That we may be filled with your love for others.
Grant us peace in our hearts, for you are our true
    peace;
Where there is peace, you yourself draw near.
Come to us, O Lord, and possess us in joy:
Make us a temple of your Holy Spirit. Amen.

The Water of Life

Jesus said, 'No one can enter the kingdom of God without being born from water and the Spirit.'

(St John 3:5)

Grant, O merciful Jesus,
That as you have graciously permitted me
To drink sweetly from your Word which tells of
    you,
To allow me in your goodness to come at last to
    you, the fountain of Wisdom, That I may stand
    before your face for ever. Amen.

(Bede)

The Cup of Salvation

When we bless the cup of blessing, is it not a means of sharing in the blood of Christ? When we break the bread, is it not a means of sharing in the body of Christ?

(1 Corinthians 10:16)

Almighty God, you caused your Son to drain to the bitter dregs
The chalice of his passion, for the redemption of your dying people.
We now call upon you and humbly ask you, the fountain of Wisdom,
To confirm us in holiness, stability of life and loving service,
By the gifts of your Holy Spirit of love.
We ask this through Jesus Christ our Lord. Amen.

The Living Bread

Jesus said, 'I am the bread of life – the living bread that has come down from heaven; if anyone eats this bread, he will live for ever. The bread that I shall give is my own flesh, given for the life of the world.'

(St John 6:48–51)

May your holy Body, Lord Jesus Christ, give me
    eternal life;
May your precious Blood give me forgiveness of all
    my sins.
May this Holy Communion bring me joy, health
    and true gladness.
Make me worthy to stand before you when you
    come again in glory,
Supported by the prayers of all your angels and
    saints. Amen.

Ambassadors for Christ

We are Christ's ambassadors. It is as if God were appealing to you through us: we implore you in Christ's name, be reconciled to God!

(2 Corinthians 5:20)

Lord Jesus Christ, the way, the truth and the life;
Let us not stray from you who are the way,
Nor distrust you who are the truth,
Nor rest in any other but you who are the life.
Teach us by your Holy Spirit
What to believe, what to do and say,
And in what to take our rest.
We ask this for your Name's sake. Amen.

(Erasmus)

The Hope of Heaven

I saw a new heaven and a new earth; and the holy city, new Jerusalem, coming down out of heaven from God, made ready like a bride adorned for her husband; and the One who sat on the throne said, 'Behold! I am making all things new!'

(Revelation 21:1–5)

Let everything in heaven rejoice and on earth be
    glad,
For the Lord has shown strength with his arm:
By death he has trampled down death;
He has become the first-born from the dead.
He has delivered us from hell and evil,
And offered to us all his mercy and the hope of
    eternal life. Amen.

PART TWO

Saints at Prayer

Introduction

The second part of the book begins with a meditative form of prayer to the Holy Spirit: it enables us to sense the work of God as a whole in the lives of Jesus and of the saints. This is followed by a special and well-loved way of praying to Jesus himself, and then some of the classic prayers which draw us closer to his mother, Mary, the first among the saints.

Some of the saints and spiritual teachers of Christianity are then introduced. Their writings will help develop and deepen our prayer and commitment to Christ as life unfolds, and there is a guide to further reading at the end of this section. There is also a timeline of all the saints whose prayers are included in both parts of this book.

Those who have gone before us on the path of love and prayer can help and encourage us in our own praying. Like stars, their light, though ancient, still streams back to us, as they themselves move further into the eternal life and love of God in heaven. They tell us that our prayers matter, for as St Gregory the

Great once said, 'Your good deeds are evident where you are, but your prayers reach where you cannot be.'

The Holy Spirit, Comforter and Guide

Let us pray to the Lord for the gift of his Holy Spirit
– the Spirit of wisdom and understanding, the Spirit
of judgement and strength, the Spirit of knowledge
and fear of the Lord.

*Come, Holy Spirit, fill now the hearts of your
faithful people:*
Kindle within us the fire of your love.

Holy Spirit of God, you brooded over the waters of
Creation, as the Light of Life: you spoke through
the prophets the wisdom of God's Law.

Kindle within us the fire of your love.

Holy Spirit of God, by your power Jesus was
conceived in the womb of Mary: you descended upon
him at his Baptism, filling him with your healing
power.

Kindle within us the fire of your love.

Holy Spirit of God, you enabled Jesus to overcome temptation and to destroy evil: you gave him strength in his final agony and suffering on the Cross.

Kindle within us the fire of your love.

Holy Spirit of God, by your mighty power Christ was raised from the dead: you descended upon the apostles in wind and fire, to give birth to the mission of the Church.

Kindle within us the fire of your love.

Holy Spirit of God, you give us new life through Baptism and Confirmation: you restore us in the image and likeness of God, through prayer and Holy Communion.

Kindle within us the fire of your love.

Holy Spirit of God, bond of love between the Father and the Son: you call us to the vision of your glory; you transfigure your saints with your eternal light.

Kindle within us the fire of your love.

Come Holy Spirit, and fill us with the fruits of your life within us – love, joy, peace, patience, kindness, goodness, faithfulness, gentleness and self-control.

Come, Holy Spirit, fill now the hearts of your faithful people: kindle within us the fire of your love.

The Jesus Prayer

The 'Jesus Prayer' has ancient roots in the monastic life of the Eastern Church, but it is now widely used by many Christians across the world. It comprises words drawn from the gospels, and it is a prayer for meditation in the heart, either silently or with the movement of breathing. It is designed to bring a person into encounter with Jesus the living Lord.

The Jesus Prayer

Lord Jesus Christ, Son of the living God:
Have mercy upon me, a sinner.

You know how we breathe the air in and out? This is the basis for the whole of our life and its warmth. So as you sit down to pray, collect your mind and let it follow your breath into the depths of your heart. Keep it there but never let it remain idle or silent: use this prayer – 'Lord Jesus Christ, Son of the living God, have mercy upon me, a sinner.'

Let this be your mind's constant occupation within your heart, for this will protect it from all suggestions of evil, and lead it through desire to the love of God. For the Kingdom of God is within us, and the person who has glimpsed or experienced this through pure prayer will find everything else loses its former attraction.

A person should always live with the Name of the Lord Jesus on the breath, so that the heart absorbs the Lord, and the Lord absorbs the heart, and the two become one. May the memory of Jesus combine with the rhythm of your breathing, and then you will discover the true value of silence before the Lord.

(Adapted from *The Philokalia*)

Saints at Prayer

The Trisagion

Holy God, Holy and Strong, Holy and Immortal, have mercy upon us.

Holy God, Holy and Strong, Holy and Immortal, have mercy upon us.

Holy God, Holy and Strong, Holy and Immortal, have mercy upon us.

Glory be to the Father, and to the Son, and to the Holy Spirit:

Both now and for ever, and unto the ages of ages. Amen.

Holy God, Holy and Strong, Holy and Immortal, have mercy upon us.

Mary – The Mother of Our Lord

From the beginning of the Church's life, Christians have identified closely with Mary, the mother of Jesus, and with the spirit of her response to God's call, recorded in the opening chapters of St Luke's gospel. They have sensed her prayers and her compassion as the mother of the Church and first among the saints. To pray to or with her is to draw close to Jesus himself.

Mary said to the angel, 'Behold, I am the servant of the Lord; may it be to me according to your word.'

(St Luke 1:38)

Hail Mary, full of grace: the Lord is with thee.
Blessed art thou among women,
And blessed is the fruit of thy womb, Jesus.
Holy Mary, Mother of God, pray for us sinners,
Now and in the hour of our death.
Pray for us, O Holy Mother of God,
That we may be found worthy of the promises of
    Christ. Amen

Almighty and everlasting God,
You stooped to raise our fallen race
By the childbearing of blessed Mary:
Grant that we who have seen your glory revealed in
    our human nature,
And your love made perfect in our weakness,
May daily be renewed by your Holy Spirit,
And conformed to the likeness of your Son, Jesus
    Christ,
Who lives with you and the Holy Spirit, one God
    for ever. Amen.

It is indeed right to hail you as blessed, who gave
    birth to Christ our God:
You are blessed for ever and most pure as the bear-
    er of God.
Your honour is higher than the cherubim,
Your glory shines more brightly than the seraphim,
For without sin you gave birth to God the Word,
And it is truly as the holy God-bearer that we love
    and praise you.

We ask you, O Lord, to pour your grace into our
    hearts:
That, as we have known the Incarnation of your
    Son, Jesus Christ,
Through the message of an angel, so through his
    Cross and passion
We may be brought to the joy and glory of his
    resurrection.
For he lives and reigns with you and the Holy Spirit
    forever. Amen.

St Augustine

St Augustine was one of the most influential Christian theologians. He lived between 354 and 430, and died as Bishop of Hippo in North Africa. These readings come from his Confessions, *which recount how he became a Christian as a young person. He was deeply moved by the love and beauty of God as revealed in Jesus Christ. His writing is the first work of Christian spiritual autobiography.*

O God, you awake us to your praise, for you have made us for yourself, and our hearts are restless until they find their rest in you. Let me know and understand which comes first – to call upon you and then to praise you, or to know you and so to call upon you? Meanwhile, I will seek you, Lord, by calling upon you, and I will call upon you by believing in you; for you have given me faith through the Incarnation of your Son, Jesus Christ, and the word of your preacher.

But how shall I call upon God, my God and my Lord, since when I call for Him I shall be inviting Him within myself? What room is there within me into which God Himself may come, who made heaven and earth? Yet I could not even exist unless you were already within me, O Lord; or more truly I found myself in you.

O eternal truth, true love, beloved eternity! You are my God, and I sigh to you day and night. You said to me: 'Grow and you shall eat me. But you shall not change me into yourself: you shall be changed into me.' It was only when I found Jesus Christ, the mediator between God and human beings, that I could receive in union with him that food which I had lacked the strength to take.

Late have I loved you, Beauty so ancient and so new; late have I loved you! For you were hidden within me while I looked for you outside myself, and in my ugliness I fell in love with those lovely things that you have created. You were within me, but I was not with you. It was you who called to me, and broke open my deafness, sending forth your beams of light to banish my blindness; and you breathed on me the fragrance of your love. I tasted you, and now I hunger and thirst for you. You embraced me, and I now burn for your peace.

St Isaac the Syrian

St Isaac lived in Iraq in the seventh century. He was a hermit, who for a brief while was bishop of Nineveh or Mosul. At the very end of his long life he dictated his spiritual teaching, which has had great and lasting influence throughout the Eastern Church. His style reflects a time when people remembered sayings of wisdom and meditated on them. He provides way-marks for our pilgrimage of prayer towards God.

The ladder to the Kingdom of God is hidden within you, and within your soul. Dive down into yourself, away from sin, and there you will find the steps by which you can ascend to God.

Thirst for Jesus so that he may fill you with his love.

Consider prayer to be the key to insight into the Truth contained in the Scriptures.

The way to God consists of bearing the Cross day by day: no one can ascend to heaven in comfort.

Just as a flowing fountain is not blocked by a handful of dust, so God's mercy is not overcome by the evil of those whom He has created.

The aim of prayer is to acquire love for God.

O Name of Jesus, key to all gifts,
Open for me the great door to your treasure house,
So that I may enter and praise you from my heart
In thanks for your many mercies.
For you have come and renewed me,
Bringing an awareness of a new world.

St Anselm

St Anselm was an Italian monk who came from the monastery of Bec in Normandy to be the second Archbishop of Canterbury after the Norman Conquest. He died in 1109, and his writings and example remained highly influential. He was a philosopher as well as a teacher of prayer, with a wonderful gift for friendship. The first two readings come from his Proslogion, *the last one is drawn from his many prayers.*

Seeking God

Come now, little man,
Turn aside for a while from your daily employment,
Escape for a moment from the tumult of your
    thoughts.
Put aside your weighty cares,
Let your burdensome distractions wait,

Saints at Prayer

Free yourself awhile for God,
And rest awhile in Him.
Enter the inner chamber of your soul,
Shut out everything except God
And that which can help you in seeking Him;
And when you have shut the door, seek Him.
Now, my whole heart, say to God,
'I seek your face; Lord it is your face I seek.'

Faith seeking Understanding

My God, I pray that I may so know you and love you
That I may rejoice in you.
And if I may not do so fully in this life,
Let me go steadily on to the day when I come to
    that fullness.
Let the knowledge of you increase in me here,
And there let it come to its fullness.
Let your love grow in me here,
And there let it be fulfilled,
So that here my joy may be in a great hope,
And there in full reality.

Lord Jesus Christ, the hope of my heart, the
    strength of my soul,
The help of my weakness;
By your powerful kindness complete
What in my powerless weakness I attempt.
You are my life, the end to which I strive.
Although I have not yet attained to love you as I
    ought,
Still let my desire for you
Be as great as my love ought to be. Amen.

St Francis

St Francis of Assisi is one of the best known and loved of Christian saints. He died in 1226 having founded a movement throughout Europe of men and women who followed his example and embraced the poverty of Christ. He taught that love of God is discovered through love and service of others.

Love your neighbour as you love yourself

We can never tell how patient or humble a person is when everything is going well with him. But when those who should help him do exactly the opposite, then we can tell. A person has as much patience and humility as he or she has then – and no more!

Love one another as I have loved you

Blessed is that person who loves his brother or sister as much when they are sick and can be of no use to him as when they are well and can be of use.

Blessed is that person who loves and respects his brother or sister when they are absent as when they are present, and who would not say anything behind their back that could not be said charitably to their face.

The Praises of God

You are love, you are wisdom.
You are humility, you are endurance.
You are rest, you are peace.
You are joy and gladness.
You are justice and moderation.
You are all our riches, and you alone suffice for us.
You are beauty, you are gentleness.
You are our protector, our guardian and defender.
You are our courage, our haven and our hope.
You are our faith, our great consolation.
You are our eternal life,
Great and wonderful Lord God Almighty,
Our most merciful Saviour. Amen.

Mother Julian

Mother Julian of Norwich lived mainly in the second half of the fourteenth century, and died some time after 1413. In 1373 she received visions of God, which laid the basis for her own spiritual life; she wrote them up many years later in her book The Revelations of Divine Love. *She believed that God's love revealed in Jesus is the key to all that exists.*

Love is our Lord's meaning

The Lord showed me spiritually how intimately he loves us. I saw that he is everything that we know to be good and helpful. In his love he clothes us, enfolds and embraces us; that tender love completely surrounds us, never to leave us. As I saw it, he is everything that is good.

And he showed me more, a little thing, the size of a hazelnut, lying on the palm of my hand, round like a ball. I looked at it thoughtfully and wondered, 'What is this?' And the answer came, 'It is all that is made.' I marvelled that it continued to exist and did not suddenly disintegrate; it was so small. And again my mind supplied the answer: 'It exists, both now and for ever, because God loves it.' In short, everything owes its existence to the love of God.

I am the foundation of your praying

Prayer unites the soul to God. However like God the soul may be in essence and nature, once it has been restored by grace, it is often unlike Him in fact because of sin. Then it is that prayer proclaims that the soul should will what God wills; and it strengthens the conscience and enables a person to obtain grace. God teaches us to pray thus, and to trust firmly that we shall have what we ask. For He looks at us in love, and would have us share in His good work. So He moves us to pray for what it is He wants to do.

So it was that I learned that love was our Lord's
  meaning.
Before ever He made us, God loved us;
His love has never slackened, nor ever shall.
In this love our life is everlasting.
All this we shall see in God for ever.
May Jesus grant this. Amen.

St John of the Cross

St John of the Cross lived in Spain between 1542 and 1591. He was a monastic reformer who was impris-oned for a while for his beliefs. While in prison he composed his Spiritual Canticle, *which enshrines a profound experience of God. He went on to describe in his other writings how contemplative prayer leads a person through definite stages to an encounter with the living God. These lines from some of his poetry and writings give a glimpse of his spiritual vision.*

In a dark night
My cares consumed by love,
O journey of delight!
Unseen by all
I sallied forth while all my home was hushed.

Secure and in disguise,
I crept up my dark and secret stair,

O blessed enterprise!
I went not knowing where,
And with no other light
But that which kindled in my heart.

It guided me so surely,
More certain than at noon,
To where He awaited me
Whose presence I know well,
In that place where no other presence can be felt.

For God secretly and quietly pours into the soul a loving knowledge and wisdom, without any active human intervention, though sometimes He may prompt specific acts of love within the soul for a while. Then the soul has to walk with a loving awareness of God, quite passively and without any active diligence of its own. Instead it possesses a simple, pure and loving sense of God, like a person that opens his eyes full of love.

(Adapted from *The Living Flame of Love*)

Michael Ramsey

Michael Ramsey was born in 1904, and was Archbishop of Canterbury from 1961 until 1974; he died in 1988. He gave great leadership to the Anglican Communion by his theology, social compassion and ecumenical commitment. He was a spiritual leader and teacher of great simplicity and depth, who had a special rapport with young people.

Being with God

It means putting yourself near God, with God, in a time of quietness every day. You put yourself with God, empty perhaps, but hungry and thirsty for Him. You can be very near to Him in your simple sincerity; and He will do the rest, drawing out from you longings deeper than you ever knew were there, and pouring into you trust and love.

Praying for others

Anywhere, everywhere, God is to be found. You can be on God's side of every human situation, for God's side is a part of every human situation. Your prayer will then become a rhythmic movement of all your powers, moving into God's presence in contemplation, and moving into the needs of other people in intercession. In contemplation you will reach into the peace and stillness of God's eternity; in intercession you will reach into the rough and tumble of the world of time and change.

Lord, take my heart and break it:
Break it not in the way I would like,
But in the way you know to be best.
And because it is you who break it,
I will not be afraid,
For in your hands all is safe,
And I am safe.

Lord, take my heart and fill it with your joy,
Not always in ways I like,

But in the ways you know are best,
That your joy may be fulfilled in me.
So, Lord, I am ready to be your friend, your
   servant. Amen.

A Timeline of Saints at Prayer

Christian prayer is very much a sense of sharing in a living past as well as a living present. This list places the saints to be found in this book in chronological order.

St John Chrysostom   + 407
   Archbishop of Constantinople
St Augustine of Hippo   + 430
   Bishop and Theologian
St Benedict of Nursia   + 550
   Abbot and Spiritual Teacher
St Gregory the Great   + 604
   Pope and Apostle of the English
St Isaac the Syrian   + 700
   Hermit and Spiritual Teacher
The Venerable Bede   + 735
   Monk and Historian
Alcuin of York   + 804
   Theologian and Educator

St Anselm of Canterbury   + 1105
  Archbishop and Philosopher
St Francis of Assisi   + 1226
  Apostle of the Poor
St Thomas Aquinas   + 1274
  Theologian and Teacher
Mother Julian of Norwich   + 1413
  Mystic and Spiritual Teacher
Erasmus of Rotterdam   + 1536
  Scholar and Writer
St John of the Cross   + 1591
  Mystic and Spiritual Writer
Evelyn Underhill   + 1941
  Spiritual Teacher and Writer
William Temple   + 1944
  Archbishop of Canterbury
Gilbert Shaw   + 1967
  Priest and Spiritual Guide
Michael Ramsey   + 1988
  Archbishop of Canterbury

Acknowledgements

Sincere thanks are due to the SLG Press, Oxford, for permission to quote from *The Face of Love*, by Gilbert Shaw, and also from *The Wisdom of St Isaac the Syrian,* with personal permission from Dr Sebastian Brock; also to Penguin Publishers and to Sister Benedicta Ward SLG for permission to quote from *The Prayers and Meditations of St Anselm*, and from Mr John Wolters for personal permission to quote from his father's translation of *The Revelations of Divine Love,* also published by Penguin Publishers; also to the Continuum International Publishing Group for permission to use some prayers from *Prayers for use with the Alternative Services.* Other permissions have been sought, and will be asked for if needed before any future editions of this book are published. This book draws on prayers accumulated for use with young people over many years of ministry, and it has not been possible to trace the origin of them all. Bible references are drawn from *The Revised English Bible.*

Further Reading about Prayer

Adam, David, *The Rhythm of Life*, London: SPCK, 1996

Barrington-Ward, Simon, *The Jesus Prayer*, Oxford: Bible Reading Fellowship, 1996

Brock, Sebastian, *The Wisdom of St Isaac the Syrian*, Oxford: SLG Press, 1997

Dales, Douglas, *Called to be Angels*, Norwich: Canterbury Press, 1998

Dales, Douglas (tr.), *Christ the Golden Blossom*, Norwich: Canterbury Press, 2001

Milner-White, Eric, *My God, My Glory*, London: SPCK, 1954

Mursell, Gordon (ed.), *The Story of Christian Spirituality*, Oxford: Lion, 2001

Palmer, G. E. H., P. Sherrard and K. Ware, *The Philokalia*, London: Faber, 1979

Pine-Coffin, R. S. (tr.), *St Augustine's Confessions*, London: Penguin, 1961

Ramsey, Michael, *Be Still and Know*, London: Fount, 1982

Futher Reading about Prayer

Ramsey, Michael, *The Christian Priest Today*, London: SPCK, 1987

Shaw, Gilbert, *The Face of Love*, Oxford: SLG Press, 1977

Silk, David, *Prayers for use at the Alternative Services*, London: Mowbrays, 1980

Theophan the Recluse, *The Path of Prayer*, ed. Robin Amis, Newbury, MS: Praxis Institute Press, 1992

Ward, Benedicta (tr.), *The Prayers and Meditations of St Anselm*, London: Penguin, 1973

Ware, Kallistos, *The Power of the Name: the Jesus Prayer*, Oxford: SLG Press, 1974

Williams, Rowan, *Ponder These Things*, Norwich: Canterbury Press, 2002

Wolters, C. (tr.), *Julian of Norwich: Revelations of Divine Love*, London: Penguin, 1966

Index of Themes

Index of Themes